Dreamers and doers,
Whiners and wooers.

The question to answer though is
Who are you?

This book is for entrepreneurs.
Like me. Like you.
To get out of this lull,
By pulling ourselves up.

This book is...
For DOERS.

Testimonial

A practical handbook, lucid enough for any entrepreneur to understand. Especially - if you can see only 10 feet ahead and if you can manage each 10 feet, you will be home! The script nicely brings out the possible mindsets of an entrepreneur & illustrates possibilities, with a good guide using the 'market map' - most will relate to it! The book is a good example of "practice what you preach" - simple communication that will impress both the expert as well as the novice.

Veerendra Mathur

Entrepreneur & Charter Member, TiE Chennai

WHY IS THE eBOOK BEING GIVEN FREE?

To help you as I am being helped.

Together!

I have one request though.

Please donate to the Bhoomika Trust, a non-profit that works towards disaster mitigation, relief and rehabilitation.

Bhoomika has launched a programme to ensure that disadvantaged daily wage earners and disadvantaged communities have enough to eat during COVID-19 regulations.

BHOOMIKA TRUST

Contributions within India:

https://www.bhoomikatrust.org/donate-for-covid/

Contributions from Abroad

Please make your tax deductible donations at:

https://deservingcauses.org

DCI supports Bhoomika Trust India

CLIMB YOUR WAY OUT OF

HELL

OUTLIER MARKETING TO OVERCOME WORST-CASE
SCENARIOS AND GROW YOUR BUSINESS

KRUX108

PRAVIN SHEKAR

INDIA · SINGAPORE · MALAYSIA

Notion Press

No.8, 3rd Cross Street, CIT Colony,
Mylapore, Chennai, Tamil Nadu – 600004

First Published by Notion Press 2020
Copyright © Pravin Shekar 2020
All Rights Reserved.

ISBN
Paperback 978-1-64919-532-6
Hardcase 978-1-64919-545-6

CONTENTS

Contents

ABOUT THE AUTHOR

Pravin Shekar is an outlier marketer and a raconteur.

Unconventional marketing is his forte. When the world moves one way, you need to move another way: that's his philosophy. This going-against-the-grain attitude helps him find opportunity in every crisis.

A recipient of the American Marketing Association's "Emerging Leader" award, Pravin has written 4 books and is set to bring out few more, on various aspects of Marketing. He is passionate about marketing and believes that micro-marketing can redefine the business environment.

When you have to shake up your marketing strategy and re-gear your growth, reach out to him at mic@pravinshekar.com & www.linkedin.com/in/pravinshekar.

The Books:
www.pravinshekar.com/publishing/

ON MARKETING

- **DEVIL DOES CARE:** Outlier Marketing for Bootstrapped Entrepreneurs
- **HOW TO GET MY FIRST PAID SPEAKING GIG!**
- **VIRTUAL SUMMIT PLAYBOOK:** A Guide to Hosting Your Own Online Conference.
- **CLIMB YOUR WAY OUT OF HELL:** Outlier Marketing to Overcome Worst-case Scenarios and Grow Your Business *(yes, the book you are holding!)*

TALK-BOOK

- OPHTHALMOLOGISTS BRAND YOURSELF!

ON CREATIVITY

- WITH YOU, FOR YOU: A Collection of Travel Images and Romantic Poems

IN THE PIPELINE

- THE GHATOTKACHA GAME: Marketing Lessons from Mythology
- LOVE IS JUST A PAGE AWAY: Short Stories from the Heart
- STREET SMART MARKETING: Marketing Lessons from the Street Vendors of Chennai

PRELUDE

The cricket match was exciting. A clash of titans. Our rivalry was generations-old. Who cared about the prize money? It was always a fight for pride and bragging rights!

We studied their videos, assessed each of their players. We had our playbook ready. The game was on, and we invited them to bat first. We loved to chase. Our bowlers played to the plan. We restricted them to a below-par score. 220 runs, when the par was 300. Our planning, did I say, was spot on? The manager, coach, captain, vice-captain, 12th man, our ball boys – were all grinning in anticipation of our win. This was going to be a cakewalk.

You know where I am leading you, right?

Our solid openers went in to bat. And were back in the pavilion before I could say "well played". The other two who followed them to the pitch came back equally soon. Heads hanging, chests shrunk. Tensions ran high. Our fans were shell-shocked, as were we. This was never the plan! We were supposed to breeze through and come back. Here we were though, with only 4 wickets in hand and needing 161 runs to win the match.

All plans gone awry, everyone froze. Hope and prayer seemed to be the only strategy left at the moment.

Forget victory, this was going to be a disgrace. A definite loss was staring at our face. Panic, fear, self-pity, silence. Each one of us just wanted to be left alone.

This cup was important for us to get into the next league.

Can someone tell us what to do? Can you send us a miracle?

What can we do now?

The situation is same in a football field, when you need to score 2 goals to win. You have 10 minutes on the clock. Your best player is tackled, injured and out of the field. The captain red-cards himself and is out. Your team is playing two men down, and praying for deliverance.

Two different games. Two not-so-different scenarios.

Thanks to Covid-19, aren't we in a similar situation now? Much worse perhaps, as this is a fight for survival. Not to play another match another day, but to even live to see another day.

In other words, a fight to get out of hell.

This hell of the unknown and invisible tyrant that has played havoc with lives and business.

Is there a way out?

This is the question in my mind and yours.

The answer is YES. Don't call me an optimist. I am a practical marketer, and I know that however difficult the situation, there is *always* a solution. My business is bleeding, as well. It has been slashed is red across, just as your business has been.

This book is for myself and my fellow entrepreneurs like you. I have interacted with over 2000 entrepreneurs in the last two months. This book throws up questions that are a constant today, ideates on them and provides options for all of us.

Why?

A cross-sea is an ocean phenomenon. A square repeating pattern appears when winds from two weather systems collide. The waves so formed cross while traveling at slanting angles to each other. Therefore, the sea becomes an extremely dangerous place for anyone out there - ship, boat or swimmer. Tall waves are visible, and therefore dangerous. But even more dangerous are the rip currents that are formed under water.

A cross-sea occurrence is rare and quite fatal for those caught in it.

We are in the midst of a global cross-sea, and we need to find a way to survive and get out to the shore.

What are we ready to do to survive?

That is the fight we are in now.

And we have long run out of excuses, as there is no status quo. But thankfully, we do have some time on our hands!

Key Takeaways from this Book

1. HOW CAN I SURVIVE THIS NONSENSE?
2. HOW CAN I PIVOT?
3. HOW CAN I GENERATE REVENUES?

This note does NOT have checklists. It also does not give you a prescription. It gives you thoughts, ideas and examples. The rest is really up to you. You are an entrepreneur. A leader.

SO, BE ONE.

ACT LIKE ONE.

How to make a business plan in the face of the pandemic?

Make a survival plan.

When you drive at night on any Indian highway, you'll see that there are no lights.

All you can see is ten feet ahead.

But that is enough for you to cover a journey of even a thousand kilometres. In the same way, for your business today, can you see ten days ahead and plan accordingly. **So, make that ten-day plan.** That will roll into the next ten and so on.

One step at a time.

Survive today. To succeed tomorrow.

As an outlier marketer, I love alternative learning. To achieve my objective, I will learn from everything around me and everything I can get my hands on. In this book therefore, I have included dialogues and learnings from movies, along with Quartiles written by me.

When the world around you is sinking,

Are you paralyzed?

Or getting ready

To take off.

GROUNDHOG DAY

It is a routine. Every day seems the same. You wake up at the same time, do the same chores. The same coffee, the same hello, the same news site, work calls and so on.

Phil Connors is caught in the same time loop on Groundhog Day. Every day is the 2nd of February for him. He hates the monotony, and tries several ways to escape it. He even tries to commit suicide, but wakes up the next morning to the same song at the same time. The day repeats itself endlessly. Isn't this similar to the lockdown some of us are stuck in?

Phil decides to make use of the routine to better himself. Every day he strives to become better, learn new skills, learn a new language and help more people. Rita falls in love with the new Phil. When he turns into a new positive Phil, he wakes up to the 3rd of February.

A milestone movie for Bill Murray.

Loads of learnings for us entrepreneurs.

This repetition of monotony has to be harnessed to learn more, plan more and do more.

Back to the wall,
Death staring at you.
Lean back, then jump forward,
As that's the only way out.

ONE

WHAT IS THIS ENTREPRENEUR HELL?

THE ENTREPRENEUR'S HELL FUNNEL

The entrepreneur's hell, a place where everything that can wrong, does. Support vanishes, the future looks bleak and we beat ourselves up in self-pity. A negative spiral, leading us deeper into a hellhole.

The only way out is to be first aware of the folly in our ways and approaches. We need to know the sins associated with us as individuals, leaders and entrepreneurs; because when we know and accept, it is easier to change.

It is then easier to CLIMB OUT OF THIS HELL.

This is not a negative book, but a practical one. One that figuratively slaps you into awakening and action.

Let us start with the entrepreneur sins.

Which of the sins shown in this illustration do you relate to? These sins are there, of course, even during normal circumstances. But they are very stark and pertinent in times of crises. When you know the sins, you will, at the very least, know what NOT to do.

Here's my retelling of Dante's Circles of Hell, customized for entrepreneurs like you and me.

GET RID OF THESE ENTREPRENEUR SINS TODAY.

First, the lighter side:

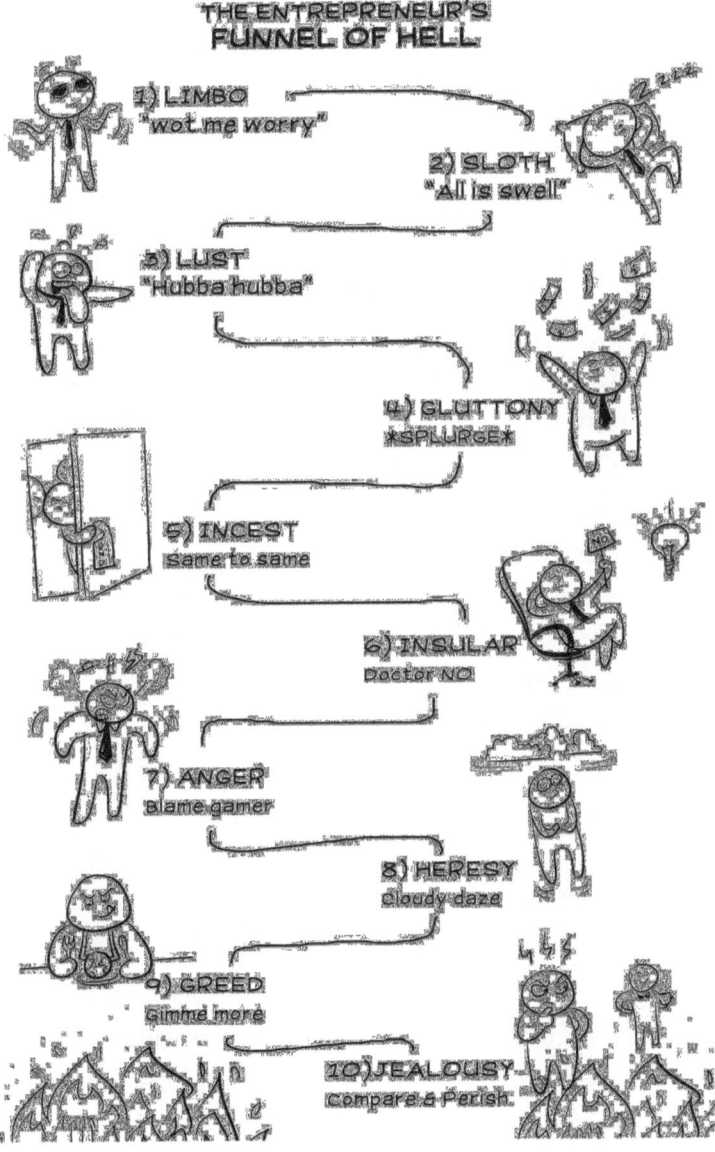

Then, the serious side:

1. **LIMBO:** Don't know there's a problem. Don't see a need to do something. If you don't understand the need and importance of marketing, well, welcome to hell.

2. **SLOTH:** The ostrich syndrome. Dig your head in and pretend there's no problem. "Everything is fine. I don't need to do anything. Why plan? What's a scenario?"

3. **LUST:** We have what we need. We need to live within that. The lockdown has taught us that. Anything more then, isn't that lust?

4. **GLUTTONY:** Spending money without measurement. Being happy with vanity metrics but having no connection with reality. Is it generating leads? Am I making money? You cannot afford to dwell in gluttony anymore. Marketing is ceasing to be the big gray area it used to be.

5. **INCEST:** I will do what I have done. It worked for me before. It will continue to work. Things will be back to normal. Incestuous: same team, same ideas, same work...

6. **INSULAR:** Insular: It wasn't developed here. So, I won't use it.

   Don't bring in new ideas. Listen to me, I know everything. I will do it myself. Boring ideas. If you are still sticking to an old template of a dated playbook, welcome to this level of hell.

The only escape is outlier thinking and marketing, where you add value and build trust.

7. **ANGER:** The client is an idiot. They don't understand me or my products. The government is to be blamed. Another country. Even gods. But not me!

8. **HERESY/RUMOURS:** It will get better. They said it. Selective hearing (and intake) is a hell in itself. Letting the self-bias cloud understanding and judgement.

9. **GREED:** I want it all. Everyone is my client. The whole world is my market...

10. **JEALOUSY:** He seems to get it all...

I am smarter than him. But I don't seem to get the same results. How can he alone.....? I will ensure he can't get it either!

MOVIE: BRUCE ALMIGHTY

You can keep complaining and blame the whole world. What happens when you accuse god of not doing a good job? What if he gives you his job to run for a week?

Bruce takes up the job of Almighty, albeit only for a small region in the US. Unable to handle the job, Bruce says yes to all wishes coming to him. The city falls into chaos and rioting. Bruce runs back to god for help, but god refuses.

God says NO!

God says he will not solve all problems and that Bruce has to sort this one out himself. Bruce tries his best. But unable to manage, he goes back to god one last time. God does relent and help him out.

In the end, Bruce goes back to his regular job, but takes pleasure in every little thing that happens. No more whining!

GET OUT OF HELL. OUT OF SCENARIO L.

WHAT ARE THE FOUR SCENARIOS WE ARE TALKING ABOUT?

The global economy continues to tank. Let's leave that aside.

Let us look at this scenario: Revenue for our business has come down. It has either slowed down or hurtled downhill. In certain cases, it has come to a standstill. There are four major scenarios of economic recovery that could be in play today. Each scenario is denoted by a letter: V, U, W and L. One of them is "hell".

I am not an economist. Therefore, this is my simplified explanation for the benefit of fellow entrepreneurs.

Let us say that a particular service is priced at 100x under normal circumstances. As the crisis continues, the rate keeps dropping. When it is at 10x, you panic and hope that this is the bottom. But what if the drop continues to 1x? What would you do? What are the possible scenarios for recovery?

Four scenarios for economic recovery are provided here with price/rate on the Y axis and time on the X axis.

V:

100x → 0x → 100x

We are at the bottom of the V, or so we hope. But we don't know.

Revenues have tumbled and the best hope we have is that they will bounce back up, and that things will be all hunky-dory, happy and normal again.

Back to business, as it were.

Keep dreaming!

SCENARIO "V"

"The Trampoline"

U:

$$100x \rightarrow 0x \rightarrow 0x \rightarrow 0x \rightarrow 100x$$

The next best-case scenario. The global financial fever will abate slowly, but it will. For sometime, everything appears to be standstill. After a while, the recovery will happen. Super-fast.

"I'll be back!" Terminator style.

Dream on.

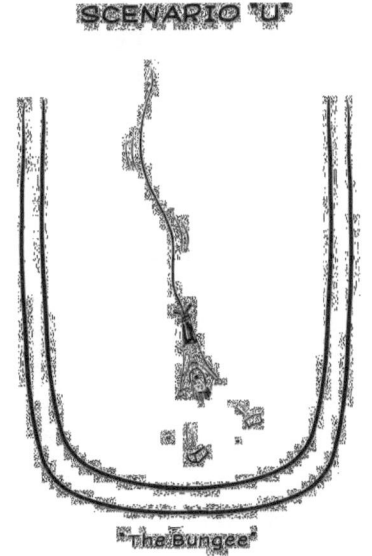

SCENARIO "U"

"The Bungee"

W:

$$100x \rightarrow 0x \rightarrow 10x \rightarrow 0x \rightarrow 30x \rightarrow 0x \rightarrow 100x$$

This will sound familiar. We were the bottom and then, the liquor shops were opened by the powers-that-be. There was an immediate uptick in sales and hangovers. And an exponential rise in Covid cases!

There was a definite upward blip.

The liquor shops were quickly shut down or their timings severely moderated. And the blip came crashing down again.

It may go up again, slightly. And horror, it may come down again.

The W merry go-round!

SCENARIO "W"

"The Roller coaster"

L:

This is the scenario that brought this book out. This L is the HELL we need to prepare for. And to climb out of!

$$100x \rightarrow 0x \rightarrow 0x \rightarrow 0x \rightarrow 0x \rightarrow 0x \rightarrow 0x \rightarrow 0x \rightarrow 0x$$

The scenario L that nobody wants to talk about. The scenario whose name will not be uttered! Well, it is here.

What was once going for 100x, is now at 0x. We can hope and pray that we've hit rock bottom and that 0x is the new normal. That is the Scenario L. If you don't accept it, it will be hell.

The flat part of the L is the new (ab)normal we need to get used to.

Ok. Then if x is what the customer is willing to pay, I cannot try to thrust my 10x solution. It just won't work.

What then do I need to do to survive in L?

Read on.

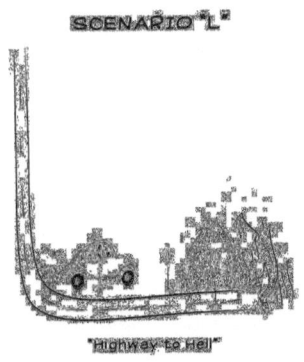

SCENARIO "L"

"Highway to Hell"

29

MOVIE: RUN LOLA RUN

What would you do if there could be multiple endings for a movie? Or for your business?

What if there exist multiple scenarios, each of which keep changing based on every move you make?

I am quoting from the book "Management Lessons from Movies" by Gokul Santhanam. He has analyzed the movie "Run Lola Run" from a scenario planning perspective. The protagonist Lola has a limited time in which to act and save her boyfriend's life.

Every action of hers spawns a different scenario track - in real time!

In the movie, she gets three chances to get it right. In reality, you and I get just one chance and very limited time.

The only way to make the most of that one chance is to invest in planning possible scenarios, our actions and potential outcomes. The key is to pick what we think is the right strategy for the scenario facing us.

When the planning is good, we will know how to respond.

NOT PREPARED

(This is an old story told in Japan.... I read it on WhatsApp. A take on Pataal Lok.)

There is a Zen story about a great samurai warrior.

One night, he comes back home and finds a very big rat sitting on his pillow. Of course, he goes mad. This is too much! An ordinary rat and so daring?

He takes his sword -- because that is the only thing he knows -- and hits the rat. But the rat escapes and sits in another place, looking at the samurai and blinking his eyes.

Now the samurai is furious. This is the first time in his life that he has missed any target, and this rat is trying to befool him.

In his madness he hits here and there, and because of his madness he goes on missing.

Suddenly, he feels a cold shiver and begins to perspire. A thought arises in his mind. This rat is no ordinary rat; there is something mysterious about it. **Maybe it is a ghost?**

Scared, the samurai rushes out of the room. He tells his family. They tell him not to be afraid and not to get so worked up. They bring their cat to the room.

The cat is brought but the samurai is still shivering and trembling. The cat looks at the samurai and gets scared.

There must be something very fearful there, otherwise why is the samurai -- such a great man and a great warrior -- so afraid?

The scared cat enters the room and the rat jumps on her. The cat escapes, shivering and perspiring.

The whole town's cats are brought in, but they look at the scared samurai and the scared cat and go blank! It seems simply impossible to catch the rat.

Then the villagers go to the palace and the king's cat is brought in. She is taken to the samurai's room.

She simply goes in, takes the rat in her mouth and comes out. All the cats gathered outside asked her, *"What is the trick?"* The king's cat replied,

"There is no trick. I am a cat and he is a rat -- finished. There is no trick."

"There is nothing to be praised. I am a cat; that's enough for me to catch the rat. He is a rat. As it is natural for me to catch him, it is natural for him to be caught."

This is exactly what we must understand in today's context.

You are an entrepreneur, you are a leader, you solve problems. You are a cat! So why be afraid of rats?

Problems will come; they are just like rats.

Situations will arise; they are just like rats.

The samurai missed because of his irrational fears.

The other cats missed because they were scared - because of the contagious nature of the 'scare' virus and irrational fears!

But the king's cat knew what had to be done and simply did it.

So can I. So can you!

When a problem arises and you are not prepared, you will be surprised how beautifully you tackle it. There is no fear or trembling, because there is no ready-made answer. You are not disturbed. You simply see the problem from all sides and do whatever it takes to solve it.

So, go as the king's cat, and you will catch many rats!

CLIMB OUT OF THE IRRATIONAL HELL.

Things are murky, yet clear as day,
Happy one moment, sad the next.
That's the state we are in,
When in love and war!

THE "GET OUT OF HELL" MARKET MAP

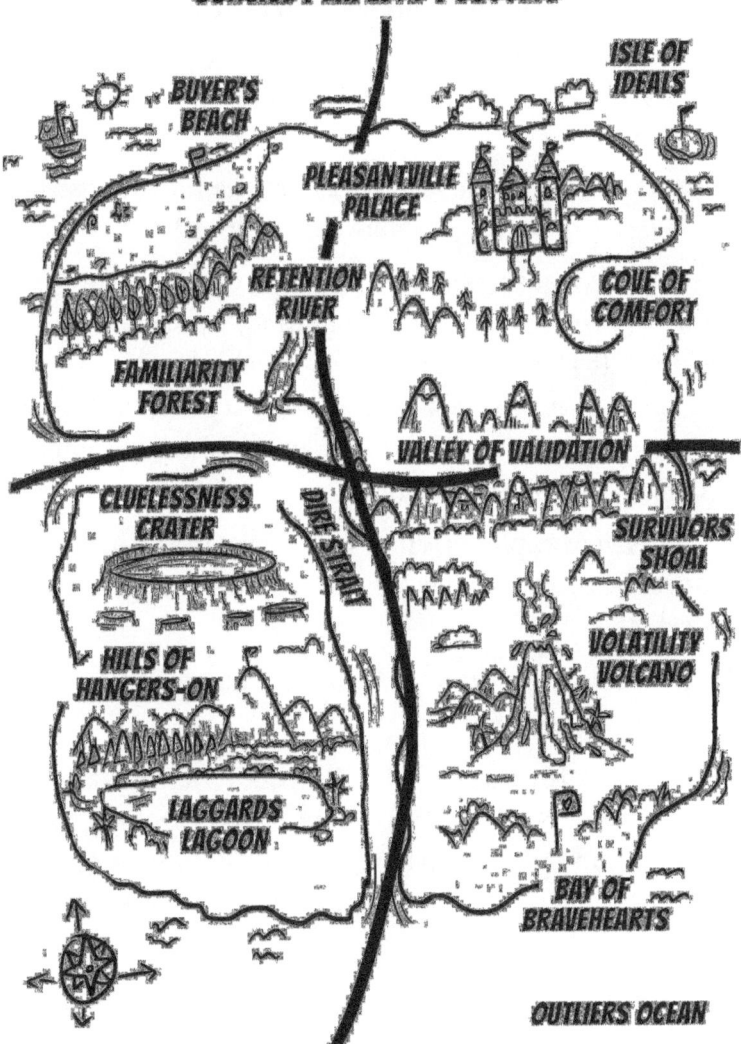

This is a business book. So, it has to have a grid! Cliché!

An outlier grid-map that shakes it all. Touché!

When you surround yourself with creative people, the outcome will be creative, too. This map was designed by Arun Ramkumar of Mojo Canvas. It underlines the fact that:

> *We should go ahead and rip apart the normal as we plan for the new (ab)normal!*

Assess where you are, with the help of the map shown here. This map is a metaphor of our business journey. It is meant to figure out where we are, our strengths, what we know and what we don't. At any point, our business divisions or initiatives lie in one of the points shown in the map.

This map explains what we are gravitating towards, naturally. It also shows where we need to move and invest.

What should we do to safeguard what we have, and increase revenues?

Look at the map again. Consider market know-how on the Y axis and buyer familiarity on the X axis. For new buyers on one side to familiar buyers on the other of X. Knowing the market above to not knowing the market of Y.

The top right quadrant is the dream area. This is where growth entrepreneurs focus under normal circumstances; the "Cove of Comfort". Some of us have been operating there or at least have a few new clients. The market in this quadrant is the first to freeze in any crisis. Decision-making will freeze, as will newer initiatives.

So, we move left to the next easy option. We focus on the "Retention River", going back to buyers we know. Clients who know us and have worked with us. Back to the basics of the "Familiarity Forest". Wooing them back. A good base to work on if you have been diligent in loving them. **This is critical**, as we need to go deeper in (re)building relationships with our clients. This is important to keep the cash flows running. This base is our foundation for survival.

The bottom left quadrant of the "Cluelessness Crater" is where the bulk of entrepreneurs and marketers wallow. The mass, the madding crowd. This is what I call the necessary death zone, the "Dire Straits". The laggards' zone. There is minimal-to-no creativity here, as it is full of copy-cats and me-toos. I wouldn't want to be caught dead in this quadrant. Nor should you.

The bottom right quadrant is the one most of the entrepreneurs run away from. Who wants to add more ambiguity to this situation? I don't know the market and I don't know the buyers. Why will I enter this segment...? The fear of the unknown! Why venture into unfamiliar areas?

Nothing comes easy. If you want to survive and get by, stick to the "Buyer's Beach" quadrant. If you want to explore, seed and succeed, go beyond the "Volatility Volcano". Yes, some initiatives will be burned but hey, we are entrepreneurs.

Think OUTLIER.

This is the best bet for new growth. You don't know the market or the buyer, but will invest in research. For you to find out about new needs, devise new solutions for a new market. More on this later, but for now, think about why you were hesitant to enter this quadrant.

THE BAY OF BRAVEHEARTS!

Everyone wants it, but they don't know where to get it from.

They don't want to enter it, as there is a huge fear of rejection.

Of failure. Of "what will people think?"

The very thought makes my stomach churn. My nostrils flare up. I have trouble breathing. My brain refuses to function. I stand there gaping.

All signs of falling in love and being stupefied with the act of proposing to someone.... Better I love from afar!

Best to stay in the quadrant where I am comfortable.

But that comfort quadrant will soon turn into a graveyard. Only those who care for their lives and the livelihoods of the associates dependent on them will move.

You've got to be one of the few who take action, who move, who explore. And survive.

Survive today, to succeed tomorrow.

Use the "Buyer's Beach" quadrant to set your survival base. From here, JUMP.

Get back on to the startup entrepreneur pilot seat. You are starting from scratch, but building on the momentum you already have. If you are at a standstill, well, then start jogging slowly! **Jump** into the "Bay of Bravehearts" quadrant in the map. New geographies, new market, new ideas and new validation → growth.

SURVIVE. EXPLORE. SUCCEED.

Use word-of-mouth references from existing clients.

Repurpose existing services and products.

Devise new solutions for a newer market need.

Network and re-connect - for connections, ideas and action!

Kill all negativity and explore!

Never reveal all your moves,
Never open your face and body.
Small fast steps and really quick jabs,
What works in boxing, works for survival.

FIGHT

How does one market a business that is unable to do business during the Covid-19 pandemic?

One does not.

This is a time to reboot and change the way we operate.

This is a time to understand existing clients and delivering value-add. What more can we do for our clients?

This is the time to either repurpose existing solutions and services OR come up with new services.

How do you keep your business safe with the help of technology during this pandemic?

Use technology to understand clients better. Use it to reach them through various modes and assist them.

Repurpose your content and answer client queries.

If you are into manufacturing, switch to products that are much required now. If you are running a physical store, use your connections to procure and delivery products your clients need now.

What are some investments that can be profitable for your businesses during this pandemic?

How do I stay in business during and after this pandemic?

You need to survive today in order to succeed tomorrow.

For this, you need to calculate your minimum revenue requirement: your break-even amount. To this end, you need to approach existing clients and secure this.

When you know "how much" clearly, the rest will follow quickly.

How should businesses be thinking about the future when it is still so unclear how we will come out of the pandemic?

Assume the worst-case scenario and plan for that. Work on what you know and are sure of. We don't know when the situation will improve. What we know is that we need to survive **until then**. What are you ready to do for that?

What is clear? Your strengths, your clients, your solutions **and the clients' needs today**.

You need to understand people, the life changes happening and the newer decision-making styles.

PEOPLE. FACTS. LIFE.

Some facts are presented below. You may even classify them under "Controversial Commonsense". You may be right.

1. **People don't like to change..** No sir, I am happy where I am. Let me be. If the product I need is not there, I will live the rest of the days fondly recalling that product. And no, don't expect me to understand you or the benefits of your solution. I will not even bother. I, me, myself and my ways. Don't you dare try to change me.

2. All I need to do is grit my teeth and wait for the wind to blow over. And if I find some sand, I will bury my head in it and be at peace. **Have you heard of the ostrich behaviour?** At the first sign of trouble, they bury their head into the sand. The problem skirts them, passes by. And the ostrich comes up again. I am an Ostrich too. Hey problem, take a detour. Please. I want my old life back.

3. The silver bullet is coming. That vaccine is around the corner. A solution is almost here. Get away, you panic mongers, negativists and pessimists. Bugger off! I will wait for that silver bullet to kill this invisible Werewolf, the virus. Poooof!

4. **DENIAL:** This word needs to be banned. This cannot be happening. Not to me. Not now. Never. How? Why? This is Maya, an illusion, a mirage, a twitch in a parallel universe.

5. **FEAR:** We need to give the enemy a shape, a name, a structure. When the enemy is invisible, there will lots of rumors around. All leading to fear. Which leads to immobility! I am scared. I don't know what will happen and you want me to what? Buy your solution? Seriously! Unless you're selling masks and vaccines, I don't need you.

6. **CHANGE:** That's the last thing I want. Why don't you understand that, O Entrepreneur? I don't need to change and if at all I do, it will be in very small, infinitesimal steps. Yeah!

These are facts that we need to deal with. Regardless of how virtual the world will become, decisions are still being made by humans. That means you have to understand the emotions of your customers - current and future. Hasn't that been the bedrock of marketing all through? Why forget that now, when we need it the most?!

The past has to give way,
For the future to come in.
The old ways need a burial,
So we can come out of denial!

MOVE

TWO

HOW CAN I SURVIVE THIS NONSENSE?

Finally, you say, I am getting around to giving some gyan. Well, I'm not. I am only writing what I am doing as an entrepreneur and a marketer.

WHAT SHOULD I DO NOW FOR MONEY?

Money saved = money earned.

What can I save now?

- **Cost:** What's the saving per employee in the work-from-home? Calculate that and factor it into your survival plan.
- **Contracts/agreements:** Renegotiate all contracts. Rental, vendors, Annual Maintenance Contracts, everything.
- **Contract:** A play on words but this lockdown has made it clear who is working and who isn't! Contract, as in right size. Evaluate everything: productivity, utilization, attitude, discipline, ability to deliver and the ability for self-leadership. Your core will emerge, quite clearly.
- **Change portfolios:** High-cost resources must be in revenue-generating activities that includes strategic leadership. Mid-level resources need to handle multiple projects. Invest in automation tools. Re-skill resources, since the need now is for generalists: people flexible to take on multiple roles as per the requirement.

- **Connect**: Grow your network, and look for collaborations and strategic partnerships. There's a time to build and buy. *Now is the time to borrow* **(resources, know-how, connections). For a couple of projects, instead of recruiting full-time resources, I "borrowed" the skills from another company where the resource was sitting idle.**

- **Community**: Build a tribe of freelancers for *just-in-time* use. Pay per project, and as per need only. In a Freelancer.com survey of approximately 20,000 respondents, 61.5% stated that going ahead, *they will be using freelancers online, instead of hiring full-time staff*.

- **Do something outlier**: Invest in key vendors and partners. Either through direct investment into their companies or by giving them forward orders. This might sound counter-intuitive, but outlier thinking always is like that. You are building a base for the future.

- Do you really need that fancy office anymore?

I repeat, money saved is money earned. And we need every paisa at the moment.

SHOULD I go behind NEW clients?

Use this three-point framework to get out of this phase.

1. CONSOLIDATE
2. TWEAK
3. PIVOT

Consolidate: RETENTION is the primary focus. Understand your existing clients a lot more. Go deeper. Identify your anchor clients. What are their issues? What value can you add? What can you do for them? Having understood all this, go ahead and *do it.*

Tweak: What can you tweak in your existing service to support existing clients? *Do it.*

Pivot: New services for old and new clients. *Sometimes, your current clients themselves may need, not your regular services but new ones at a time like this. So, I think when you pivot, you must consider offering new services to your old AND new clients.*

We shall cover all three in this book.

Should I keep the price high or drop?

If necessary, drop the price to retain customers.

And use the price drop to bring in new customers.

I would rather work at a lower price than do zero work.

One big loss is that of revenue. The other bigger loss is that rust settles in. When you don't exercise, muscle gets replaced by fat. When you don't work on your core, rust settles in. You may become slower or in the worst case, forget how to do things effectively. So, keep taking on work, keep bettering your skills and your craft. Survive today, to succeed tomorrow.

Do whatever is necessary to stay afloat, to keep working, to keep fires burning.

Who can help me now?

Who will not?

This is the time to strengthen your relationship with your NETWORK.

Talk to your clients, old and new. Ask what they are up to. What problems they are facing. And how you can help.

Remember, everyone is a lot more available in times of crisis. People are looking forward to connecting to others. Are you connecting enough? Are you listening enough? ACTIVELY.

Use your current clients to get introductions to new prospects. It is effective networking that will convert an introduction to a strong referral. Build those relationships now.

GIVE. ADD VALUE.

And ASK.

Is it really Important to experiment with new ideas?

Hmmm. YES. This question is important at all times. Whether there is a crisis or not, you must experiment with new ideas. All the time. Especially NOW. Form your ideation team and execute the ideas.

Which types of businesses will be the first to rebound from the COVID-19 economic crisis?

The entrepreneur who is ready with scenario planning, understands the immediate his clients' needs and has a plan to cater to those asap – that business will rebound much before the crisis passes us.

The entrepreneur who already has a set of clients, however small, will rebound faster.

What do you think will be the main changes we will see in business and society as a result of the pandemic?

In the immediate term, buying and consumption patterns will change. Non-contact services will have a better chance to succeed. Also, the NEED will have a lot more focus than the WANTS.

What specific things will you need to stop doing or let go of?

WHO AM I and what do I want?

You know who you are and what you need to survive. Write it down and quantify clearly how much money you need. This is something you need week on week, month on month.

EVALUATE THE PEOPLE AROUND YOU

When I started writing my first book (after several aborted attempts), this is what my book coach Kiruba Shankar told me.

Surround yourself with your real friends. When you announce that you are writing your first book, check the reaction of those around you. When someone makes fun or ridicules you and discourages you, drop them from your circle. Note those who are positive and encouraging, and who will be ready to break your fall, when required. This small group becomes the people you surround yourself with.

This was true for book-writing. My small group has been active now for over five years. This group continues to push everyone in it, to push boundaries, to do more.

As you plan on getting the hell out of L, you need positive people around you. You need DOERs around you. People to inspire and people to look up to. There are enough pessimists and naysayers in the world. I don't want them anywhere near me. Nor should you.

What I need are ideators, alternative thinkers, creative people. Those are the people I want to meet regularly, to discuss with and use as a sounding board. I need to survive. I need people who will jump into the water to save me, not those who stand by on the shore, shouting instructions to me!

BE CAREFUL ABOUT THE PEOPLE AROUND YOU: Board of Directors, team, friends, partners, allies.

Pick them carefully – and give them more than you get from them.

EVALUATE: This includes your employees and associates. The work-from- home model removes all wrappers. It is easy to identify the doers.

You're my love, my support,
You understand me and I, you.
In these moments of strife, there for each other,
You client, me vendor; you associate,
me entrepreneur;
as we partner together, ahead!

LOVE

IF IT IS WORKING NOW, ASSUME IT ISN'T.

Planning for scenario L, if it isn't broken, break it anyway.

Write down the doomsday scenario.

For example:

What will you do if your revenue drops to zero?

What will you do with the additional staff sitting idle in your company?

What if your anchor client and their business are being severely impacted by a crisis?

This note is to goad you to assume the worst, write it down as scenarios and plan for it.

Yes, the plan may not work just the way you write it down. But you will know how to react and what to do. This has been thought through, by you and your team. It is clear what needs to be done.

GO ON THE OFFENSIVE.

SPECIFICALLY, GO TO WAR.

Warfare. That's what we are involved in now.

War against an invisible enemy, whose effects are clearly visible and far-reaching.

This is no time to fall back. This is the time to go on the offensive.

Whoever was earlier competition for you and me, well, they are also in the same plight as us today. This virus war is a great leveler, that way. We are all almost equals.

What will you do to be the first among equals?

I will go to war. I encourage you to, as well.

When fighting a bigger enemy whose size and strength you are not yet aware of, you convert the war into many smaller battles.

Battles that you can play in your war zone, in your territory. Smaller skirmishes, smaller projects and trials, smaller wins and even smaller losses. Guerrilla warfare, all to win a small piece of land. In our case, a small amount of necessary revenue. Customer acquisition, one at a time. These dots all connect to the bigger war for survival.

Instead of waiting for the effects to impact you, act on it right now.

YOU ARE THE STRONGEST when you have nothing in hand.

This is our restart from zero – our reboot.

MOVIE: THE DARK KNIGHT RISES

What's the first step?

Let me retell a scene from the movie, The Dark Knight Rises.

Batman is injured, and is a prisoner in an underground cell. The only way to escape the jail is to climb a well and make a daring jump. This jump is beyond any normal human being. It is suggested that only one person has done it before. A boy. The stuff of legends.

Several people attempt the jump, safety ropes and all. Only to bite the dust. Batman tries as well, to fail. Until he decides to go all outlier. He refuses to use the safety ropes. He decides he will risk it all, including death.

Stunned silence all around, as everyone watches him. He pauses, looks at the distance and takes off. To escape. To survive. And succeed.

He cut off the safety rope.

That's the first step. Knock off your crutches, leanings and support.

This is war.

CUT OFF WHATEVER SAFETY ROPES ARE THERE.

Physically, and in the mind!

IT IS A MENTAL GAME

It always has been.

Regardless of the glamour around valuations and market sizing, it has always been a mental game. How strong are you, internally, really? Are you a real entrepreneur or a fair-weather one? When the weather is fair, anyone can take on the leadership and coast along. When the going gets tough, when the shit hits the fan, *when the ship is sinking* - the rats are the first to leave.

What are you?

This book is for DOERS. Those who want to survive. Those ready to do whatever it takes in a crisis. We are cornered and desperate. If we don't act now, when will we ever?

All sins are in the mind, then the body. Sinful somethings keep me busy!

Walk trot gallop canter,
That's the way of the horse.
We've become babies again
Horse around we must, for growth and survival.

THREE

HOW CAN I PIVOT?

MOVIE: THE PURSUIT OF HAPPYNESS

Living in homeless shelters and in railway stations, Chris Gardner has a kid to take care of. Zero money in his pocket. He lives a day-to-day existence, barely surviving.

He manages to get an unpaid internship that he must succeed in to get a confirmed job. He has limited work time and so he goes all in. Desperation drives him.

He must succeed. He maximizes client contacts and comes up with a number of ways to make the sales calls more effective. He reaches out to potential clients and builds a relationship. He connects with prospects outside the regular norms of interaction.

He knows what he needs to do. He needs wins. And he makes it happen.

WHATEVER IT TAKES!

HOW DESPERATE ARE YOU?

THIS SECTION will have a lot of questions. Only questions. For entrepreneur examples, read on to the next section.

Remember: CONSOLIDATE, then PIVOT.

IDENTIFY

What is it that you do? For whom? What is the need that you are satisfying? How is the client satisfying that need now?

What is your requirement? What is your monthly financial need to break even? Which is the customer segment that is most loyal to you? Which is most profitable?

Write it all down, include all data that is available.

ASSESS

Entrepreneurs who do not understand their customers are "Asses"! The purpose of this section though, is to find out where you are, and what the current need is.

Look at the data:

Is there a need for your solutions now? If yes, how much?

If no, then what are your strengths? What can you use to repurpose for a new client segment?

PRICE: How much are they willing to pay? How much are you willing to drop?

It is better to drop your rates and keep the clients, than letting another competitor in. When the market is better, the clients will remember your assistance.

QUANTIFY:

What is the core need of your clients?

What is the potential of embraced usage (not just one time)?

What is the overall market viability?

RESEARCH & IDEATE

Form an ideation team and do a virtual meeting. The ideation team has to go beyond friends and family. Get an external moderator to assist unbiased idea sessions and outcomes.

State your objective clearly: **How can I earn this much per month?** This is what I have with me (strength, resources).

What can I do?

Do I repurpose my solution or design a new one?

What are the new client segments I can serve? Why should my solution be of use to them? What can I do to make them aware of my existence?

How are they currently using different solutions?

How can I generate revenue? New clients, new geographies, new solutions...

Make a long list of ideas. Prioritize on the basis of practicality and capability to generate immediate revenues.

EXPLORE MICRO-PRODUCTS

Whatever your new service or product idea is, can you offer/implement it in smaller circles? Ideation to proof-of-concept to prototype to testing with live clients. Call it agile or quick loops, micro-products are the way to go. It helps you connect with ideal clients/ users and co-create your solution.

Let's assume: You have been going behind clients who were paying $100,000 per deal. In a crisis, the appetite is not there anymore. Can your service be broken down to chunks that can be priced at $10,000? In such a case, you need to bring in ten clients.

Or

You can design a new solution that is priced at a bite-sized level, that fits the need and the paying appetite of your prospects.

TO PIVOT OR NOT

The strategy of a long-distance runner,
Doesn't apply to a sprinter.
The moves of a mass advertiser,
Rarely apply to a micro-marketer

You pivot when:

a. the traditional revenue stream has dried up.

b. competition is heating up, making your solution a commodity.

c. when the economy isn't supporting you.

Tick all three for the current climate.

What isn't a pivot?

A logical progression of business as it grows is not a pivot. That is *evolution*. If your business is offline, then moving online is a natural growth move. It cannot be classified a pivot.

Gentle nudges and pushes also do not constitute a pivot.

What is a pivot?

A pivot is a fundamental shift in using your strengths to arrive at new solutions for old or new client segments. When the old is not working, it needs to make way for the new.

As defined by a book called "The Lean Startup", a pivot is

"A structured course-correction designed to test a new fundamental hypothesis about the product, strategy, and engine of growth."

Guess these companies:

This company started as a video dating service. People could upload short videos to describe an ideal partner. This business idea didn't take off. So, the founders used what they had and pivoted to offer a completely different service.

This company started with a goal to create a camera platform with a cloud portion for storing photos online, and for smart cameras to connect to PCs. This company also pivoted.

The first example is YouTube, while the second is Android OS.

ACTION TESTING

Once you have identified 2-3 new ideas and segments, you need to hit the market fast. Test it with live clients in an agile manner. Is it working? Is it solving their need? Do they like it? Will they use it continuously? Do they love it? Do they love it so much that they will market it to their circle?

TWEAK

If it isn't working, check what can be tweaked. You have tested it in a small market. Is the idea wrong? Timing wrong? Or the selected client segment wrong?

Give the idea some more time before you write it off.

If it works, then...

SCALE

If it works, check how it can be scaled. One client or one micro- segment at a time.

FASTEST FINGER FIRST

It's ok to be wrong.

It is **not ok** to be silent and **not do anything.**

The market needs solutions. You need to be out there providing it (for your client segment).

Again, plan for being wrong and write down how you will handle it.

Tweak, run the next circle, measure, scale.

F A S T.

When the whole world is in muck,
The stink will not be noticeable.
Everyone's trying different things,
The question is, are you?

DIFFER

FOUR

WHO HAS DONE IT (recently)?

Some examples of companies that are pivoting are given below. These are meant to spur your creativity, and push you to explore and do more.

KATHA108 as a producer

Katha108 was launched as a startup on February 1, 2020. This was aimed at repurposing videos from speakers into smaller content bytes. This content could then be shared across channels to increase the tribe and build a following.

March 2020. Covid struck and business tanked.

April 2020. Katha108 re-emerged as a content creator, curator and producer. Two books have been brought out, with ten more in the pipeline. A video album, a meditation music album, a cookbook, a travel photo coffee-table book and two marketing games. They are all now part of the "new avatar" production, for new clients across geographies.

Collaboration with designers and game developers. Retraining of resources and adding fresh talent. A startup reborn (with paying clients).

MYHARVEST: Service extender

MyHarvest connects farmers to urban buyers in a way that makes the buyers feel like "urban farmers". A startup that has proven the business model and is on the growth path. When the lockdown hit, MyHarvest could get the necessary passes, as they delivered vegetables.

Their clients wanted more.

Myharvest got in touch with fruit producers and egg hatcheries. They already had the delivery routes planned out, and so, just added more products to their roster.

Their clients were happy. So were the farmers and producers!

Address the need. Add value across the customer journey.

Farm to home, fresh.

It will not work here,
It cannot be done.
That's not the way we do things,
Time to wipe the slate clean and start afresh.
Mentally!

REBOOT

KUMAR SYSTEMS AND SERVICES: EXTEND!

Ramesh's business installs closed circuit security TVs (CCTVs). CCTV planning and installation is their forte, and they do a good job of it. The bulk of their growth is through word-of-mouth recommendation from existing customers.

Ramesh stays in touch with his clients and keeps track of their needs. He uses WhatsApp as a communication medium and personalizes each message.

When lockdown hit, he took a month off. Then, he bounced back and approached his existing clients. He offered them laptops for purchase or rent, keyboards and headphones. All the electronic equipment necessary to work from home effectively!

He used his connections with dealers and vendors. He knew the current need. And he played the role of connector.

CAVINKARE: Superfast new product development

The FMCG giant realized this is a new game. A part of their revenues had dropped, as it has for most of us.

But within 21 days, CavinKare went from thought to "product on the retail shelves". They came out with a brand-new hand sanitizer brand to address the phenomenal demand.

Yes, you can argue that they had the financial muscle. But the point here is that they saw a need, repurposed their factory and retrained their resources. And they got a product out in record time!

Something each of us must emulate, in our limited capacities, in record short time!

The sanitizer is available in single-use sachets. Repurposing to the max!

What works for you needn't work for me,
I would happily assess though, and copy.
Add my imprint and make yours mine,
In this fight together, to use whatever works.

COPY

RAVI DILSEBOL: QUICK FEET AND FAST FINGERS

Continuing from the previous example, DiSeBol is a leader in corporate gifting. Ravi always does things differently. Ravi and I met a few years ago at a conference. Two days later, I received a package which had a collared tee shirt with my company logo embroidered. It fit me perfectly. Attached with the package was a letter in which Ravi requested me to check the quality of the Tee and place orders for the rest of my office! It is difficult to keep such entrepreneurs down for long.

As offices think about re-opening slowly, there is a need to have contactless hand sanitizer units. DilSebol has come out with a branded stand which can hold sanitizers and is foot-operated.

A requirement today – a clear need.

A solution they have sourced for their existing clients – and branded it with the company logo!

This was Ravi's message with the image: *Never miss a branding opportunity! Custom logo-printed foot sanitizers now available - talk to us to place your orders.*

Well, order your stand today at www.DilSeBol.com.

A FACE MASK: A NEED AND A WANT!

Reviving a closed-down non-essential service: that was the problem Binesh Paul faced, as did many entrepreneurs.

What can be done to convert his service into addressing an essential need (or want, as you see it)?

Binesh found the answer when he went out to shop for essentials. People he knew could not recognise him! If he had this issue, so will many others. How can this issue be solved?

A mask is a need, an essential commodity. As is the want to be recognised and known!

Binesh owned a photo studio and a print centre. His business included printing on mugs and tee shirts. He thought why not print the face onto a mask and sell it as a customised product? Converting a want into a need and solving a problem he himself had.

A customer comes in with a picture or Binesh takes a picture. The top of the picture is cut off, and the rest is printed on a mask. The wearer puts it on and there! You have an almost-full face - enough to be clearly recognised. All under fifteen minutes!

This timely thought and action has Binesh processing orders for 8,000 masks. He has since expanded to custom-printing of cartoon characters and saree designs onto face masks.

A need to a want to a fashion accessory – what a journey!

Source: https://www.indiatoday.in/trending-news/story/kerala-photo grapher-makes-masks-with-your-face-printed-on-it-price-just-rs-60-1682369-2020-05-27

THE LOCALXO SUNDAY MARKET: TOGETHER AT HOME. A LIMITED-TIME OFFER!

During lockdown, the yearning for specific dishes is always there, though not all ingredients are available. We pass time then, just thinking about the dish and drooling! The focus in a lockdown is more on home-cooking and DIY (do it yourself).

Where can customers get the local brands they want?

That was the idea behind the LocalXO Sunday market devised by Suneethi Raj. While a customer can order stuff via Dunzo or similar delivery services, they rarely shop from multiple places. Those visiting grocery stores have access to the regular commercial brands, but not the small, local manufacturers.

Home-delivery of a multi-vendor hamper of artisanal products in a streamlined manner solves the "wants" of a specific target audience. The idea is simple: to provide a platform that connects local niche vendors to their target audience. Most of these customers are used to the local vendors.

The target segment is clear. The want is explicit. And the products are made-to-order, based on confirmed orders.

By partnering with local vendors and providing a simplified sales platform, LocalXO is adding value to its partners and customers. All parties concerned are relieved of the burden of complicated logistics!

All products are made with an eye on DIY, which is big at the moment.. Products are made interactive, and the customers are encouraged to play around and post their results! Examples of interactivity include: A cupcake delivered with a frosting cone and sprinkles, so that kids can DIY; a ready-to-fry phyllo samosas and a ready-to-bake quiche.

Listen to the market. Change your solution model to add value, and serve that micro-market. Collaborate with like-minded partners and make things happen!

Add value, build trust. Climb your way to profitability.

PROFESSIONAL SPEAKING: Pivot & Enhance

Professional speaking, as a career, was brought to a grinding halt by the Covid crisis. No physical events meant no speaking opportunities. Overnight, a lot of speakers lost their source of revenue.

This is the time to look back, look within and plan the next course of action.

What is it that professional speakers do?

Speak, of course.

More importantly, speakers are catalysts evangelizing a forward movement, making positive change happen. They are thus messengers and knowledge disseminators.

When looked at as knowledge disseminators, what other avenues are open?

Writing books, speaking virtually, conducting webinars, opening a consulting division and coaching leaders: these are some of the options.

A simple change in thought process opens up a vista of opportunities.

And this is what Srijata Bhatnagar capitalized on. She speaks on Setback Leadership and here she was, facing a setback herself! She evaluated the situation and quickly launched an online course and online coaching to help people find their speaking niche. She is now working on her second book, to add more value to her tribe.

Sangeetha and Babu, both speakers in Finance, collaborated to convert their offline workshops to online ones. Though you cannot call these pivots, it is important to note the speed with which they brought about change.

All towards adding value, building trust, adding clients and generating revenue.

A little bit of this, a little bit of that,
A smile here and a pat there.
Little by little, inch by inch,
Add loads of value, and win clients one by one.

INCH

EXETER: Build your own stage

The London book fair cancelled their physical event, as did several other publishing conferences.

Ravi from Exeter wanted to launch their product KriyaDocs at these conferences.

Exeter therefore pivoted from attending conferences to organizing their own online conference. They launched www.publisherspeak. com and invited their clients, partners and associates across the globe to participate in this conference.

They took charge and took action. And now, they have loads of solid content, apart from goodwill and leads from clients!

GEETA KALE

This episode happened much before the pandemic, but it is a superb example of outlier marketing. The source of this story is the media coverage it received. I am retelling it my way.

Geeta Kale was devastated. She had lost a job today.

Geeta was a domestic help in Pune and was working in 3 to 4 houses. She needed this money (her income) for her family. She was sincere, and formed an easy working relationship with her clients. She was quick, efficient and effective.

Dhanashree Shinde, one of Geeta's clients, returned to her house to find Geeta crying. In between sobs, Dhanashree found out the reason. Geeta needed the job and the money.

With her marketing background, Dhanashree got thinking. The geographical area that Geeta could work in, was limited. How can awareness be created? How can I help her get another job soon?

There was also the issue of trust. Domestic help is generally in a transient, floating mode. Only once trust is established is a longer agreement is in place. Dhanashree called her friends and extended family, but none of them needed domestic help. All standard questions were answered: Who is she, what does she do, what do the services cost, what are her timings...

Dhanashree slept on this matter. And woke up with a start in the middle of the night. She quickly created a visiting card for Geeta.

A visiting card for a domestic help?! Why not?

A brilliant outlier activity.

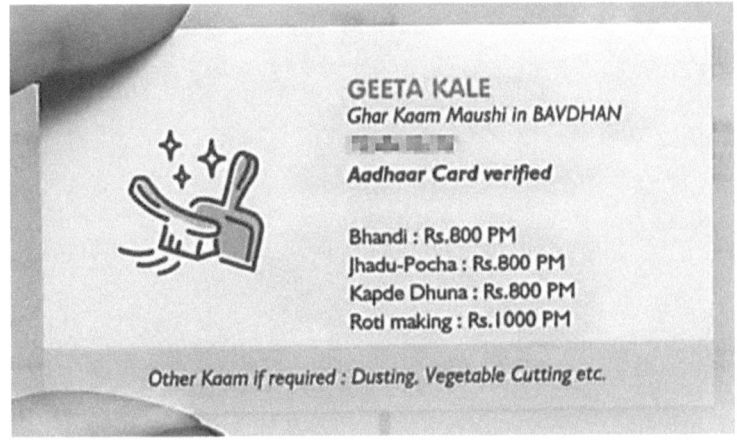

GEETA KALE
Ghar Kaam Maushi in BAVDHAN

Aadhaar Card verified

Bhandi : Rs.800 PM
Jhadu-Pocha : Rs.800 PM
Kapde Dhuna : Rs.800 PM
Roti making : Rs.1000 PM

Other Kaam if required : Dusting, Vegetable Cutting etc.

The visiting card had all relevant details about Geeta, including her Aadhaar card details. After all, it is about establishing trust from the beginning.

A price list of her work, her contact details and additional services - it was all there on that small visiting card.

Awareness and trust.

And the viral mix. A picture of this visiting card went viral on social media. Overnight, Geeta Kale became an internet sensation. Her phone wouldn't stop ringing. Just Google "Geeta Kale" or "Geeta maushi" and check out the results.

She did get another job to compensate for the one she lost. So, mission definitely accomplished!

What outlier marketing activity will you think of, for your business?

The trickle of sweat as it moves,
From the nape of the neck down the spine.
That drop finds a path, snaking down,
As will you, for survival.

FIVE

NEXT STEPS

WHAT THE HECK, ACTION TIME.

WHAT DO I HAVE TO LOSE?

What do you have to lose? We are at the bottom of Scenario L, with some businesses either down or on the verge of going out.

A cornered tiger is at its most dangerous.

A cornered entrepreneur is at his/her most creative!

A golden opportunity for all of us to reboot and restart.

I've loved, will love again,
I've been rejected, will receive many more.
Falling down, standing up, only to fall,
That's life and work intertwined, and I smile on!

RETENTION: ANCHOR CLIENTS

CONSOLIDATE. TWEAK. RETAIN.

A client in hand is worth many more in the bush!

Who are your anchor clients? What is their current status? What problems are they facing? What can you do to retain them?

One way to retain them is to find out their problems and proactively offer assistance. If you are my vendor and you help me get more clients, I will value you more. If this makes sense, what can you do to enhance your clients' (and in some cases, your vendors') revenue opportunities?

Where necessary, rework the payment terms and amounts.

VALUE-ADD

What content/connections can you come up with to help your clients?

What additional solutions can you offer them?

THINK FOR THEM.

THEY WILL THANK YOU AND THINK OF YOU.

There is always something more,
That I can do.
To show I know,
To show I care.

10 FANS

When looking for new clients, look for 10 clients (or less). Go deeper in understanding their needs and building a strong relationship with them. Go micro here. Leave mass marketing for now, however glamourous it may sound.

10 fans. Grow them a little bit more. Deliver awesome service. Make them fall in love with you.

Can they be your super fans and extended marketing arms?

I will love more,
Those who love me more.
Love is circular,
And self-sustaining!

JUGAAD: The number 8 mentality

Sleep is when the brain is resting,
Coma is when it is fighting for survival.
Easy to mistake the two,
Where are you?

KEEP CHALLENGING THE BRAIN.

SOLUTIONS WILL APPEAR.

Different different.

Think, act and do different!

What's the number 8 all about?

A concept from New Zealand, similar to that of *jugaad* in India. This was brought to my attention by professional speaker and global traveller Kiruba Shankar. An 8mm wire that seems to provide all possible solutions to work and life in general, in New Zealand. Lots has been written about the number 8 solution!

From Wikipedia: Number 8 wire was the preferred wire gauge for sheep fencing; so remote farms often had rolls of it on hand, and the wire would often be used inventively to solve mechanical or structural problems.

What do I take from the number 8?

It's a mentality. That of an entrepreneurial mind which is honed to find ingenuous solutions to business problems (and every other practical problem, as well). A mentality that identifies the crux of a problem and finds the best possible solution, given all the constraints at hand.

What is the relevance to marketing, more so to survival?

In the grand scheme of things, the CEO dream and vision, the ambition to rule the world, we forget the small steps that lead to the tall peak.

We over-complicate the mission's objectives and try to bite on a lot more than what we can chew.

The solution is already within, or around us!

Applying the 8mm rule:

Find a need. Solve the problem. Locally. With ingenuity. DO IT NOW!

Then build on top of it. And build some more. And sell. And scale.

You want a million customers - start with one, ten... there is no quick fix.

What is it that we have in abundance - but don't know about...?

Creativity: To identify what needs to be done and how best to get things done to fill that need!

And yes, of course, action beats all grand visions.

CAMBODIAN IRON FISH

Rural Cambodia had a problem. A serious problem. There was a major prevalence of anemia in the region. Iron tablets were not taken due to the negative side effects.

Something needed to be done immediately.

A Canadian student, Christopher Charles, came up with the idea of adding real iron to the food. This is not new; this has been going on for years. Iron utensils for cooking do their bit to add iron to the human body.

Christopher came up with a simple alternative. He gave away small blocks of iron for the villagers to drop into the cooking pot. The iron would release slowly into the food.

Didn't work!

The villagers thought the blocks were ugly and also scratching the cooking pots. They found a better use for it as doorstoppers and to prop up furniture.

Chris persevered. He wanted to help with the core objective of lowering the rate of anemia in rural Cambodia.

He had to make it work. He looked around and observed the local culture in more detail. Everything seemed to revolve around nature. And fish. Fish is all around them. Fish feeds them. Fish plays an important part of their culture!

Fish. The locals think that a particular type of fish brings them luck, good health and well-being.

Iron and this fish. Christopher convinced all those who needed convincing and came out with iron fish castings. Instead of giving out iron blocks, he cast the iron in the form of a fish, complete with scales!

With folklore and culture behind him, his second attempt at adding iron to the food was a super success.

The people it was meant for, adopted it and started adding the iron fish when preparing meals.

This is a classic case of alternative thinking and application in order to reach the objective.

What are YOU thinking about?

What new actions are you going to implement?
TODAY.
NOW.

When pissed with a loved one,
Silent treatment works wonders.
I dare not try that in a business setting,
As the silence echoes back!

Keep the communication on,
All the time.
Say it as you should,
All the time.

CLOSE

FORKS IN THE ROAD

The villain has kidnapped the heroine. He and his gang are hiding in a warehouse. The hero finds out and goes to rescue the heroine.

Before entering the warehouse, the hero and his army throw in sound and smoke grenades from all sides.

The villain and his gang are suffocating - eyes blinded, nose blocked - and unable to assess any sound! Total chaos and confusion inside the warehouse. That is when the hero and his team storm in, easily rescue the heroine and capture the villains.

LET US REVERSE the situation.

The hero is hiding inside the warehouse, surrounded by the villains. The villains throw in smoke and sound bombs. The hero, though, is prepared. He has practiced all these maneuvers and knows what to do. The first clink of the grenade hitting the floor, the hero and his team cover their eyes, ears and nose, and lie down. They wait for the smoke to clear, and then retaliate.

SAME STORY CORE: Two different reactions.

This is not the only crisis. We will be faced with many more.

How prepared are we? Do we know what to do in different situations?

By planning for different possible crises, and mentally and physically training for them, we ready ourselves.

When we reach a fork in the road, when a decision point comes, when we need to decide whether to go left or right: we know what to do. And we do it!

DOERS BREW MORE DOERS.

MOVIE: PAY IT FORWARD

Can you change the world? Can you make your area a better place to live?

Big goals need not be complicated. Keep things simple, make it easy to communicate. Simpler messages are understood easily and passed on to a wider network. Trevor, a 7th grade boy in the movie "Pay it Forward", comes up with a simple plan.

His plan is based on the networking of good deeds. He invites a person to do a good deed. The recipient of the favor has to pay it forward by doing a favor to three others. And so, the chain continues.

Global change is possible, one favor at a time.

Multiplied thrice.

Pay it forward by sharing this book and your learnings to the entrepreneurs who need them. Request the recipients to pay them forward to three others and keep the chain alive.

LINE UP AT THE STARTING LINE, ALL WARMED-UP AND READY TO ROLL.

WHENEVER THE GUN SOUNDS!

THIS IS YOUR RACE.

YOUR OWN.

SINCERE THANKS TO

My writing, review and encouragement team:

Gokul Santhanam

Arun Ramkumar

Ganesh Vancheeswaran

Arun Ramkumar

Dorai Thodla

Srijata Bhatnagar

Avinash Sethi

TNC Venkatarangan

Harish Kumar (OutdeBox)

Sangeeta Shankaran Sumesh

Aashik from UBC

Akhila from TiE Chennai

Archana from ASCENT

Babu Krishnamoorthy from IFA GALAXY

My trust group, The Pioneers

Nandita Pandey from Rotary Vyaapar

Narendran from Furniture Club

Sivarajah from NativeLead

My team at Krea and Krux108

Amma, Anu, Priya, Shreya & Shraddha.

If you have more questions,

stories about pivots or

would like to share certain points

where you disagree with me ☺,

please write to me at mic@pravinshekar.com.